THE
YEAR
COMES
ROUND

Haiku through the Seasons

For my wife, Wendy, my three children, Dan, Rose, and Jacob,
and my grandson, Vinny. — S.F.

For Stephanie Johnson, Gioia Sosi Tentori,
Horace Gibson, and Karen Nelson Hoyle — I.P.

Library of Congress Cataloging-in-Publication Data

Farrar, Sid.
The year comes round : haiku through the seasons / Sid Farrar ;
illustrated by Ilse Plume.
p. cm.
ISBN 978-0-8075-8129-2
1. Haiku, American. 2. Months—Juvenile poetry.
3. Nature—Juvenile poetry. I. Plume, Ilse. II. Title.
PS3606.A733T94 2012
811'.6—dc23
2011015478

The design is by Nick Tiemersma.

For more information about Albert Whitman & Company,
Please visit our web site at www.albertwhitman.com

THE
YEAR
COMES
ROUND

Haiku through the Seasons

Sid Farrar

illustrated by Ilse Plume

Albert Whitman & Company • Chicago , Illinois

Each windowpane's a

masterpiece, personally

signed: Your Friend, Jack Frost

Snowmen stand very
still, hoping the noon sun won't
notice they are there

Wily robin asks

earthworm back to her nest to

meet her family

The morning rain bursts

dandelions from the earth like

countless little suns

Surprised by her new

webbed feet, tadpole considers

a career on shore

Like tiny fallen

stars, fireflies quietly blink

their secrets at dusk

Thick, black clouds grumble

at giving up water to

the parched earth below

A mystery how

these endless rows of corn can

agree on their height

Apples loll beneath

emptying branches, dreaming

cider and hot pie

Waiting patiently

in the pumpkin patch for his

face: Jack O' Lantern

Lawns call a truce with

mowers and slip beneath their

white blankets to sleep

Brown bear politely

offers to surrender his

den to nosy skunk

HAIKU

Haiku (pronounced "hi KOO") is a form of poetry.

A haiku is made up of just three lines, with five syllables in the first line, seven in the second, and five again in the third. (A syllable is the smallest unit we hear when we sound out the parts of a word—for example, hai-ku has two syllables.)

Haiku are almost always about the natural world and usually are set in a season or month of the year. Haiku also use nature images to depict the changes in the four seasons over the year.

The haiku in this book follow the twelve months that make up each year according to the Gregorian calendar, which is commonly used around the world today.

The first recorded haiku date back to eighteenth century Japan.

THE CYCLE OF LIFE

A year is the time it takes for the earth to go around the sun. The earth is the third planet from the sun and orbits it every 365 to 366 days, the number of days in a year. At the same time that the earth is circling the sun, it also spins around once every twenty-four hours, which is how we measure a day.

Long before we used today's twelve-month calendar, people marked the passage of time by the change of seasons—winter, spring, summer, and fall. The seasons are experienced differently on different parts of the planet. People north of the equator, the imaginary line around the middle of the earth, get to enjoy more dramatic changes in the weather, flora, and fauna than people in the mostly warmer southern hemisphere.

The haiku in this book depict little vignettes in the natural world to describe these changes across the seasons and months of the year.

WINTER

Winter begins in late December and lasts through early March in the northern hemisphere. That is when precipitation and air moisture turn ce and snow as the air temperature falls below zing. Ice can form on plants and on smooth aces like the glass in windows where patterns of stals can take magical shapes, such as the storied te that came to be called Jack Frost. As the snow ins to melt, often with warmer days starting in February and early March, the birds that had grated south in the fall return to their summer nes and begin to look for food to feed their ng.

SPRING

As April arrives, the snow turns mostly to rain, alternating with bright sunlit days that grow longer as May turns to June. Leaves appear on trees and plants spring up and flower from the seeds that have found fertile soil on forest floors, prairies, and lawns. Eggs that fish and frogs have laid in underwater weeds hatch and swim to the surface of lakes and ponds, looking for food. Tadpoles lose their tails and grow legs that carry them onto the shore where they breathe air as mature frogs. By the end of June, insects have filled the air—bees dance, butterflies flutter, and fireflies blink their bellies— looking for food and mates to carry on the next generation.

SUMMER

July days are often the longest and hottest of the year. When clouds become heavy enough with water to produce rain, there can be violent storms with ctric discharges resulting in lightning. In turn, ntning causes the disturbance in the air that we r as thunder. The rain nourishes the soil in fields w filled with maturing crops like oats, wheat, and n that had been planted in spring and that will harvested in fall. In September, harvest of crops h as fruit trees begins. Fruit not harvested will fall the ground and, along with the stalks and vines behind in farmers' fields, will decay and add trients to the soil, enriching it for new growth in ing the following year.

FALL

The harvesting of many crops such as corn, soybeans, and pumpkins generally happens in October. Days cool and shorten and, with the exception of evergreens, the leaves of many trees and bushes turn various shades of orange, red, yellow, and brown and fall off. As October turns to November, birds and Monarch butterflies fly back to the warmth of the South, and rain turns to snow. Fields and lawns, now brown and covered with fallen leaves, turn white as snow deepens, and many animals store food and seek shelter from the cold— some settling into dens for a winter's sleep.

Earth circles the sun

spinning a tapestry of

days, months, seasons—life.